This journal belongs to

....

Psalms Journal

© 2008 Ellie Claire Gift & Paper Corp.
www.ellieclaire.com

Compiled by Barbara Farmer and Marilyn Jansen
Designed by Lisa & Jeff Franke

ISBN 978-1-934770-22-1

Printed in China

Psalms

journal

Ellie Claire

gift & paper expressions

...inspired by life

Praise to the Lord!

Praise the Lord!
For He has heard my cry for mercy.
The Lord is my strength and shield.
I trust Him with all my heart.
He helps me, and my heart is filled with joy.
I burst out in songs of thanksgiving.

PSALM 28:6-7 NLT

You changed my sorrow into dancing.
You took away my clothes of sadness,
and clothed me in happiness.
I will sing to You and not be silent.
Lord, my God, I will praise You forever.

PSALM 30:11-12 NCV

The Lord lives!
Blessed be my Rock!
Let the God of my salvation be exalted.

PSALM 18:46 NKJV

May the words of my mouth
and the meditation of my heart
be pleasing in Your sight,
O Lord, my Rock and my Redeemer.

PSALM 19:14 NIV

04/04/10

Praise to the Lord!

Dear G.C., Please let help me
to transfer my trust to you
100%. I want to be in the
wheelbarrow on the tight-
rope. help me to choose
actions & words that are
pleasing to you! when
I do these things my life
is truly changed, but
somehow I am tempted
& cannot see your will.
please open my eyes &
& let me see not what
I want, but your will
for me.

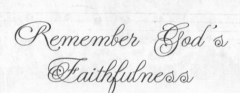

Remember God's Faithfulness

I will remember the deeds of the Lord;
yes, I will remember Your miracles of long ago.
I will meditate on all Your works
and consider all Your mighty deeds.
Your ways, O God, are holy.
What god is so great as our God?
You are the God who performs miracles;
You display Your power among the peoples.
With Your mighty arm You redeemed Your people,
the descendants of Jacob and Joseph.

PSALM 77:11-15 NIV

*G*ive thanks to the Lord, for He is good!
His faithful love endures forever.
Give thanks to the God of gods.
His faithful love endures forever.
Give thanks to the Lord of lords.
His faithful love endures forever.
Give thanks to Him who alone does mighty miracles.
His faithful love endures forever.

PSALM 136:1-4 NLT

Remember God's Faithfulness

Oh God! Thank you for all
the wonders of this world!
I want to recognize you
in all of them & always
remember that all good
things come from you.
Whenever I question
your love for me all
I will have to do is look
at this world that you
created. You & knew
me before my parents
thought of me & you
have a perfect plan
for my life. I want
to be able to recognize
all these things

Delight in the Lord

Delight yourself in the Lord;
And He will give you the desires of your heart.
Commit your way to the Lord,
Trust also in Him, and He will do it.
He will bring forth your righteousness as the light
And your judgment as the noonday.

PSALM 37:4-6 NASB

Then my soul will rejoice in the Lord
and delight in His salvation.
My whole being will exclaim,
"Who is like You, O Lord?
You rescue the poor from those too strong for them,
the poor and needy from those who rob them."

PSALM 35:9-10 NIV

I will extol the Lord at all times;
His praise will always be on my lips.
My soul will boast in the Lord;
let the afflicted hear and rejoice.
Glorify the Lord with me;
let us exalt His name together.

PSALM 34:1-3 NIV

Delight in the Lord

Desiring God

For a day in Your courts is better than a thousand outside.
I would rather stand at the threshold of the house of my God
Than dwell in the tents of wickedness.

PSALM 84:10 NASB

Lord, I cry out to You.
I say, "You are my protection.
You are all I want in this life."

PSALM 142:5 NCV

Teach me Your way, O Lord;
I will walk in Your truth;
Unite my heart to fear Your name.
I will give thanks to You, O Lord my God, with all my heart,
And will glorify Your name forever.

PSALM 86:11-12 NASB

I lift my hands to You in prayer.
As a dry land needs rain, I thirst for You.

PSALM 143:6 NCV

Desiring God

Walk with the Lord

Oh, the joys of those who do not
follow the advice of the wicked,
or stand around with sinners,
or join in with mockers.
But they delight in the law of the Lord,
meditating on it day and night.
They are like trees planted along the riverbank,
bearing fruit each season.
Their leaves never wither,
and they prosper in all they do.

PSALM 1:1-3 NLT

Lead me in the right path, O Lord....
Make Your way plain for me to follow.

PSALM 5:8 NLT

How blessed are those whose way is blameless,
Who walk in the law of the Lord.
How blessed are those who observe His testimonies,
Who seek Him with all their heart.

PSALM 119:1-2 NASB

Walk with the Lord

Planted in the House of the Lord

The righteous shall flourish like a palm tree,
He shall grow like a cedar in Lebanon.
Those who are planted in the house of the Lord
Shall flourish in the courts of our God.
They shall still bear fruit in old age;
They shall be fresh and flourishing,
To declare that the Lord is upright;
He is my rock, and there is no unrighteousness in Him.

PSALM 92:12-15 NKJV

Turn your back on evil,
work for the good and don't quit....
Live this way and you've got it made....
The good get planted on good land
and put down healthy roots.

PSALM 37:27-29 THE MESSAGE

How joyful are those who fear the Lord—
all who follow His ways!
You will enjoy the fruit of your labor.
How joyful and prosperous you will be!

PSALM 128:1-2 NLT

Planted in the House of the Lord

....

....

....

....

....

....

....

....

....

....

....

....

....

....

....

....

....

....

....

Bless the Lord

No wonder my heart is glad, and I rejoice.
My body rests in safety.
For You will not leave my soul among the dead
or allow Your holy one to rot in the grave.
You will show me the way of life,
granting me the joy of Your presence
and the pleasures of living with You forever.

PSALM 16:9-11 NLT

Salvation belongs to the Lord.
Your blessing is upon Your people.

PSALM 3:8 NKJV

Behold, bless the Lord,
All you servants of the Lord,
Who by night stand in the house of the Lord!
Lift up your hands in the sanctuary,
And bless the Lord.
The Lord who made heaven and earth
Bless you from Zion!

PSALM 134:1-3 NKJV

Bless the Lord

My Provider

The eyes of all look expectantly to You,
And You give them their food in due season.
You open Your hand
And satisfy the desire of every living thing....
The Lord is near to all who call upon Him,
To all who call upon Him in truth.
He will fulfill the desire of those who fear Him;
He also will hear their cry and save them.

PSALM 145:15-16, 17-19 NKJV

God remembered us when we were down,
His love never quits....
Takes care of everyone in time of need.
His love never quits.

PSALM 136:23, 25 THE MESSAGE

Sing to the Lord with thanksgiving....
Who prepares rain for the earth,
Who makes grass to grow on the mountains.
He gives to the beast its food,
And to the young ravens that cry.

PSALM 147:7-9 NKJV

My Provider

You Are My Strong Tower

Hear my cry, O God;
listen to my prayer.
From the ends of the earth I call to You,
I call as my heart grows faint;
lead me to the rock that is higher than I.
For You have been my refuge,
a strong tower against the foe.
I long to dwell in Your tent forever
and take refuge in the shelter of Your wings.

PSALM 61:1-4 NIV

Blessed be God, my mountain,
who trains me to fight fair and well.
He's the bedrock on which I stand,
the castle in which I live,
my rescuing knight,
The high crag where I run for dear life,
while He lays my enemies low.

PSALM 144:1-2 THE MESSAGE

You Are My Strong Tower

Bless the Lord,
O My Soul

Bless the Lord, O my soul,
And all that is within me, bless His holy name.
Bless the Lord, O my soul,
And forget none of His benefits;
Who pardons all your iniquities,
Who heals all your diseases;
Who redeems your life from the pit,
Who crowns you with lovingkindness and compassion;
Who satisfies your years with good things,
So that your youth is renewed like the eagle.

PSALM 103:1-5 NASB

Hallelujah! Praise God from heaven,
praise Him from the mountaintops;
Praise Him, all you His angels,
praise Him, all you His warriors,
Praise Him, sun and moon,
praise Him, you morning stars;
Praise Him, high heaven,
praise Him, heavenly rain clouds;
Praise, oh let them praise the name of God.

PSALM 148:1-5 THE MESSAGE

Bless the Lord, O My Soul

Proclaim His Justice

Give great joy to those who came to my defense.
Let them continually say, "Great is the Lord,
who delights in blessing His servant with peace!"
Then I will proclaim Your justice,
and I will praise You all day long.

PSALM 35:27-28 NLT

For the word of the Lord is right and true;
He is faithful in all He does.
The Lord loves righteousness and justice;
the earth is full of His unfailing love.

PSALM 33:4-5 NIV

God, Your justice reaches to the skies.
You have done great things;
God, there is no one like You.

PSALM 71:19 NCV

The Lord works righteousness
and justice for all the oppressed.

PSALM 103:6 NIV

Proclaim His Justice

Our Forgiving and Compassionate Father

The Lord is compassionate and gracious,
Slow to anger and abounding in lovingkindness.
He will not always strive with us,
Nor will He keep His anger forever.
He has not dealt with us according to our sins,
Nor rewarded us according to our iniquities.
For as high as the heavens are above the earth,
So great is His lovingkindness toward those who fear Him.
As far as the east is from the west,
So far has He removed our transgressions from us.
Just as a father has compassion on his children,
So the Lord has compassion on those who fear Him.

PSALM 103:8-13 NASB

A father to the fatherless, a defender of widows,
is God in His holy dwelling.

PSALM 68:5 NIV

Our Forgiving and Compassionate Father

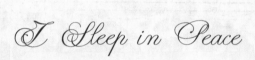

I Sleep in Peace

Lord, be kind to us.
But You have made me very happy,
happier than they are,
even with all their grain and new wine.
I go to bed and sleep in peace,
because, Lord, only You keep me safe.

PSALM 4:6-8 NCV

I cried to the Lord with my voice,
And He heard me from His holy hill.
I lay down and slept;
I awoke, for the Lord sustained me.

PSALM 3:4-5 NKJV

It is no use for you to get up early
and stay up late,
working for a living.
The Lord gives sleep to those He loves.

PSALM 127:2 NCV

I Sleep in Peace

Helper of the Needy

[The Lord] raises the poor from the dust
And lifts the needy from the ash heap,
To make them sit with princes,
With the princes of His people.
He makes the barren woman abide in the house
As a joyful mother of children.
Praise the Lord!

PSALM 113:7-9 NASB

I will give repeated thanks to the Lord,
praising Him to everyone.
For He stands beside the needy,
ready to save them from those who condemn them.

PSALM 109:30-31 NLT

The Lord protects those of childlike faith;
I was facing death, and He saved me.
Let my soul be at rest again,
for the Lord has been good to me.
He has saved me from death,
my eyes from tears,
my feet from stumbling.
And so I walk in the Lord's presence
as I live here on earth!

PSALM 116:6-9 NLT

Helper of the Needy

The Lord Is My Shepherd

The Lord is my shepherd;
I shall not want.
He makes me to lie down in green pastures;
He leads me beside the still waters.
He restores my soul;
He leads me in the paths of righteousness
For His name's sake.
Yea, though I walk through the valley of the shadow of death,
I will fear no evil;
For You are with me;
Your rod and Your staff, they comfort me.
You prepare a table before me in the presence of my enemies;
You anoint my head with oil;
My cup runs over.
Surely goodness and mercy shall follow me
All the days of my life;
And I will dwell in the house of the Lord
Forever.

PSALM 23:1-6 NKJV

The Lord Is My Shepherd

_____

_____

_____

_____

_____

_____

_____

_____

_____

_____

_____

_____

_____

The Lord's Enduring Faithfulness

Praise the Lord, all you nations.
Praise Him, all you people of the earth.
For He loves us with unfailing love;
the Lord's faithfulness endures forever.
Praise the Lord!

PSALM 117:1-2 NLT

I have talked about Your faithfulness and saving power.
I have told everyone in the great assembly
of Your unfailing love and faithfulness....
Let Your unfailing love and faithfulness always protect me.

PSALM 40:10-11 NLT

He gives food to those who fear Him;
He always remembers His covenant.
He has shown His great power to His people
by giving them the lands of other nations.
All He does is just and good,
and all His commandments are trustworthy.
They are forever true,
to be obeyed faithfully and with integrity.

PSALM 111:5-8 NLT

The Lord's Enduring Faithfulness

_____

_____

_____

_____

_____

_____

_____

_____

_____

_____

_____

_____

_____

_____

_____

Sing for Joy

May the nations be glad and sing for joy,
for You rule the peoples justly
and guide the nations of the earth.

PSALM 67:4 NIV

Shout joyfully to God, all the earth;
Sing the glory of His name;
Make His praise glorious.
Say to God, "How awesome are Your works!
Because of the greatness of Your power
Your enemies will give feigned obedience to You.
All the earth will worship You,
And will sing praises to You;
They will sing praises to Your name."

PSALM 66:1-4 NASB

I will praise You with the harp
for Your faithfulness, O my God;
I will sing praise to You with the lyre,
O Holy One of Israel.
My lips will shout for joy
when I sing praise to You—
I, whom You have redeemed.

PSALM 71:22-23 NIV

Sing for Joy

Your Word, Our Joy

Direct me in the path of Your commands,
for there I find delight.

PSALM 119:35 NIV

I inherited Your book on living; it's mine forever—
what a gift! And how happy it makes me!
I concentrate on doing exactly what You say—
I always have and always will.

PSALM 119:111-112 THE MESSAGE

The law of the Lord is perfect,
reviving the soul.
The statutes of the Lord are trustworthy,
making wise the simple.
The precepts of the Lord are right,
giving joy to the heart.
The commands of the Lord are radiant,
giving light to the eyes.
The fear of the Lord is pure,
enduring forever.
The ordinances of the Lord are sure
and altogether righteous.
They are more precious than gold,
than much pure gold;
they are sweeter than honey,
than honey from the comb.

PSALM 19:7-10 NIV

Your Word, Our Joy

Angels Watching Over Me

For you have made the Lord, my refuge,
Even the Most High, your dwelling place.
No evil will befall you,
Nor will any plague come near your tent.
For He will give His angels charge concerning you,
To guard you in all your ways.
They will bear you up in their hands,
That you do not strike your foot against a stone.

PSALM 91:9-12 NASB

God has set His throne in heaven;
He rules over us all. He's the King!
So bless God, you angels,
ready and able to fly at His bidding,
quick to hear and do what He says.
Bless God, all you armies of angels,
alert to respond to whatever He wills.

PSALM 103:19-21 THE MESSAGE

The angel of the Lord encamps around those who fear Him,
and He delivers them.

PSALM 34:7 NIV

Angels Watching Over Me

I Lift Up My Eyes

I will lift up my eyes to the mountains;
From where shall my help come?
My help comes from the Lord,
Who made heaven and earth.
He will not allow your foot to slip;
He who keeps you will not slumber.
Behold, He who keeps Israel
Will neither slumber nor sleep.

PSALM 121:1-4 NASB

Those who trust the Lord are like Mount Zion,
which sits unmoved forever.
As the mountains surround Jerusalem,
the Lord surrounds His people
now and forever.

PSALM 125:1-2 NCV

The righteous cry, and the Lord hears,
And delivers them out of all their troubles.
The Lord is near to the brokenhearted,
And saves those who are crushed in spirit.

PSALM 34:17-18 NASB

I Lift Up My Eyes

Give God the Glory

Open your mouth and taste, open your eyes and see—
how good God is.
Blessed are you who run to Him.
Worship God if you want the best;
worship opens doors to all His goodness.

PSALM 34:8-9 THE MESSAGE

Ascribe to the Lord, O mighty ones,
ascribe to the Lord glory and strength.
Ascribe to the Lord the glory due His name;
worship the Lord in the splendor of His holiness.

PSALM 29:1-2 NIV

Give to the Lord the glory He deserves!
Bring your offering and come into His courts.
Worship the Lord in all His holy splendor.
Let all the earth tremble before Him.
Tell all the nations, "The Lord reigns!"
The world stands firm and cannot be shaken.
He will judge all peoples fairly.

PSALM 96:8-10 NLT

Give God the Glory

The Blessing of Family

Behold, children are a gift of the Lord,
The fruit of the womb is a reward.
Like arrows in the hand of a warrior,
So are the children of one's youth.
How blessed is the man whose quiver is full of them.

PSALM 127:3-5 NASB

The counsel of the Lord stands forever,
The plans of His heart from generation to generation.

PSALM 33:11 NASB

Our children and their children
will get in on this
As the word is passed along
from parent to child.
Babies not yet conceived
will hear the good news—
that God does what He says.

PSALM 22:30-31 THE MESSAGE

Your children will bring you much good,
like olive branches that produce many olives.
This is how the man who respects the Lord
will be blessed.

PSALM 128:3-4 NCV

The Blessing of Family

Rescue Me

In You, O Lord, I have taken refuge;
Let me never be ashamed.
In Your righteousness deliver me and rescue me;
Incline Your ear to me and save me.
Be to me a rock of habitation to which I may continually come;
You have given commandment to save me,
For You are my rock and my fortress.
Rescue me, O my God, out of the hand of the wicked,
Out of the grasp of the wrongdoer and ruthless man,
For You are my hope;
O Lord God, You are my confidence from my youth.
By You I have been sustained from my birth;
You are He who took me from my mother's womb;
My praise is continually of You.

PSALM 71:1-6 NASB

Rescue Me

A Humble Faith

My heart is not proud, O Lord,
my eyes are not haughty;
I do not concern myself with great matters
or things too wonderful for me.
But I have stilled and quieted my soul;
like a weaned child with its mother,
like a weaned child is my soul within me.
O Israel, put your hope in the Lord
both now and forevermore.

PSALM 131:1-3 NIV

Every king in all the earth will thank You, Lord,
for all of them will hear Your words.
Yes, they will sing about the Lord's ways,
for the glory of the Lord is very great.
Though the Lord is great, He cares for the humble,
but He keeps His distance from the proud.

PSALM 138:4-6 NLT

The Lord takes delight in His people;
He crowns the humble with salvation.

PSALM 149:4 NIV

A Humble Faith

My Heart Is Confident in You

Be good to me, God—and now!
I've run to You for dear life.
I'm hiding out under Your wings
until the hurricane blows over.
I call out to High God,
the God who holds me together.
He sends orders from heaven and saves me....
God delivers generous love,
He makes good on His word.

PSALM 57:1-3 THE MESSAGE

My heart is confident in You, O God;
my heart is confident.
No wonder I can sing Your praises!....
I will wake the dawn with my song.
I will thank You, Lord, among all the people.
I will sing Your praises among the nations.
For Your unfailing love is as high as the heavens.
Your faithfulness reaches to the clouds.
Be exalted, O God, above the highest heavens.
May Your glory shine over all the earth.

PSALM 57:7-11 NLT

My Heart Is Confident in You

Lord of the Heavens

The Lord does whatever pleases Him
throughout all heaven and earth,
and on the seas and in their depths.
He causes the clouds to rise over the whole earth.
He sends the lightning with the rain
and releases the wind from His storehouses.

PSALM 135:6-7 NLT

Give thanks to Him who made the heavens so skillfully.
His faithful love endures forever.
Give thanks to Him who placed the earth among the waters.
His faithful love endures forever.
Give thanks to Him who made the heavenly lights—
His faithful love endures forever.
the sun to rule the day,
His faithful love endures forever.
and the moon and stars to rule the night.
His faithful love endures forever.

PSALM 136:5-9 NLT

Lord of the Heavens

You Have Done Many Miracles, Lord

I waited patiently for the Lord.
He turned to me and heard my cry.
He lifted me out of the pit of destruction,
out of the sticky mud.
He stood me on a rock
and made my feet steady.
He put a new song in my mouth,
a song of praise to our God.
Many people will see this and worship Him.
Then they will trust the Lord.
Happy is the person
who trusts the Lord....
Lord my God, You have done many miracles.
Your plans for us are many.
If I tried to tell them all,
there would be too many to count.

PSALM 40:1-5 NCV

Many are the afflictions of the righteous,
But the Lord delivers him out of them all....
The Lord redeems the soul of His servants,
And none of those who trust in Him shall be condemned.

PSALM 34:19, 22 NKJV

You Have Done Many Miracles, Lord

Your Lovingkindness

Your lovingkindness, O Lord, extends to the heavens,
Your faithfulness reaches to the skies.
Your righteousness is like the mountains of God;
Your judgments are like a great deep
O Lord, You preserve man and beast.
How precious is Your lovingkindness, O God!
And the children of men take refuge in the shadow of Your wings.
They drink their fill of the abundance of Your house;
And You give them to drink of the river of Your delights.
For with You is the fountain of life;
In Your light we see light.
O continue Your lovingkindness to those who know You,
And Your righteousness to the upright in heart.

PSALM 36:5-10 NASB

Lord, show us Your love, and save us.

PSALM 85:7 NCV

Your Lovingkindness

Praise the Lord Daily

Every day I will bless You,
And I will praise Your name forever and ever.

PSALM 145:2 NKJV

I will sing of Your power;
Yes, I will sing aloud of Your mercy in the morning;
For You have been my defense
And refuge in the day of my trouble.

PSALM 59:16 NKJV

Seven times a day I praise You
for Your fair laws.

PSALM 119:164 NCV

Sing praises to the Lord, you who belong to Him;
praise His holy name.
His anger lasts only a moment,
but His kindness lasts for a lifetime.
Crying may last for a night,
but joy comes in the morning.

PSALM 30:4-5 NCV

Praise the Lord Daily

God Reigns Over the Nations

For God is the King of all the earth;
sing to Him a psalm of praise.
God reigns over the nations;
God is seated on His holy throne.
The nobles of the nations assemble
as the people of the God of Abraham,
for the kings of the earth belong to God;
He is greatly exalted.

PSALM 47:7-9 NIV

With Your power You forced the nations out of the land
and placed our ancestors here.
You destroyed those other nations,
but You made our ancestors grow strong.
It wasn't their swords that took the land.
It wasn't their power that gave them victory.
But it was Your great power and strength.
You were with them because You loved them.

PSALM 44:2-3 NCV

Blessed is the nation whose God is the Lord.

PSALM 33:12 NIV

God Reigns Over the Nations

God's Constant Presence

You are all around me—in front and in back—
and have put Your hand on me....
Where can I go to get away from Your Spirit?
Where can I run from You?
If I go up to the heavens, You are there.
If I lie down in the grave, You are there.
If I rise with the sun in the east
and settle in the west beyond the sea,
even there You would guide me.
With Your right hand You would hold me.
I could say, "The darkness will hide me.
Let the light around me turn into night."
But even the darkness is not dark to You.
The night is as light as the day;
darkness and light are the same to You.

PSALM 139:5, 7-12 NCV

God's Constant Presence

_____

_____

_____

_____

_____

_____

_____

_____

_____

_____

_____

_____

_____

_____

_____

The Voice of the Lord

The voice of the Lord is over the waters;
the God of glory thunders,
the Lord thunders over the mighty waters.
The voice of the Lord is powerful;
the voice of the Lord is majestic.

PSALM 29:3-4 NIV

The waters saw You, O God;
The waters saw You, they were in anguish;
The deeps also trembled.
The clouds poured out water;
The skies gave forth a sound;
Your arrows flashed here and there.
The sound of Your thunder was in the whirlwind;
The lightnings lit up the world;
The earth trembled and shook.
Your way was in the sea
And Your paths in the mighty waters,
And Your footprints may not be known.

PSALM 77:16-19 NASB

The Voice of the Lord

The Lord Directs Our Path

The Lord will work out His plans for my life—
for Your faithful love, O Lord, endures forever.

PSALM 138:8 NLT

All the days planned for me
were written in Your book
before I was one day old.

PSALM 139:16 NCV

I will instruct you and teach you in the way you should go;
I will guide you with My eye.

PSALM 32:8 NKJV

Let the morning bring me word of Your unfailing love,
for I have put my trust in You.
Show me the way I should go,
for to You I lift up my soul.

PSALM 143:8 NIV

The Lord Directs Our Path

He'll Carry Your Load

"Who will give me wings," I ask—
"wings like a dove?"
Get me out of here on dove wings;
I want some peace and quiet.
I want a walk in the country,
I want a cabin in the woods.
I'm desperate for a change
from rage and stormy weather....
I call to God;
God will help me.
At dusk, dawn, and noon I sigh
deep sighs—He hears, He rescues.
My life is well and whole, secure
in the middle of danger....
Pile your troubles on God's shoulders—
He'll carry your load, He'll help you out.
He'll never let good people
topple into ruin.

PSALM 55:5-8, 16-17, 22 THE MESSAGE

He'll Carry Your Load

I Lift Up My Soul

To You, O Lord, I lift up my soul.
O my God, I trust in You;
Let me not be ashamed;
Let not my enemies triumph over me.
Indeed, let no one who waits on You be ashamed;
Let those be ashamed who deal treacherously without cause.
Show me Your ways, O Lord;
Teach me Your paths.
Lead me in Your truth and teach me,
For You are the God of my salvation;
On You I wait all the day.

PSALM 25:1-5 NKJV

You're my place of quiet retreat;
I wait for Your Word to renew me...
I lovingly embrace everything You say.

PSALM 119:114, 119 THE MESSAGE

I Lift Up My Soul

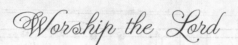

Worship the Lord

The Lord is the great God,
the great King above all gods.
In His hand are the depths of the earth,
and the mountain peaks belong to Him.
The sea is His, for He made it,
and His hands formed the dry land.
Come, let us bow down in worship,
let us kneel before the Lord our Maker;
for He is our God
and we are the people of His pasture,
the flock under His care.

PSALM 95:3-7 NIV

Exalt the Lord our God,
And worship at His footstool—
He is holy.

PSALM 99:5 NKJV

I will worship toward Your holy temple,
And praise Your name
For Your lovingkindness and Your truth;
For You have magnified Your word above all Your name.
In the day when I cried out, You answered me,
And made me bold with strength in my soul.

PSALM 138:2-3 NKJV

Worship the Lord

He Never Lets You Down

Here's the story I'll tell my friends when they come to worship,
and punctuate it with Hallelujahs:
Shout Hallelujah, you God-worshipers;
give glory, you sons of Jacob;
adore Him, you daughters of Israel.
He has never let you down,
never looked the other way
when you were being kicked around.
He has never wandered off to do His own thing;
He has been right there, listening.

Psalm 22:22-24 the message

He heals the brokenhearted
And binds up their wounds.

Psalm 147:3 nkjv

Your thoughts—how rare, how beautiful!
God, I'll never comprehend them!
I couldn't even begin to count them
any more than I could count the sand of the sea.
Oh, let me rise in the morning and live always with You!

Psalm 139:17-18 the message

He Never Lets You Down

God is Good

Praise the Lord!
Oh give thanks to the Lord, for He is good;
For His lovingkindness is everlasting.
Who can speak of the mighty deeds of the Lord,
Or can show forth all His praise?
How blessed are those who keep justice,
Who practice righteousness at all times!
Remember me, O Lord, in Your favor toward Your people;
Visit me with Your salvation,
That I may see the prosperity of Your chosen ones,
That I may rejoice in the gladness of Your nation,
That I may glory with Your inheritance.

PSALM 106:1-5 NASB

You are my God, and I will give You thanks;
You are my God, and I will exalt You.
Give thanks to the Lord, for He is good;
His love endures forever.

PSALM 118:28-29 NIV

God is Good

The Lord Counsels Me

Lord, You have assigned me my portion and my cup;
You have made my lot secure.
The boundary lines have fallen for me in pleasant places;
surely I have a delightful inheritance.
I will praise the Lord, who counsels me;
even at night my heart instructs me.
I have set the Lord always before me.
Because He is at my right hand,
I will not be shaken.

PSALM 16:5-8 NIV

God, You have taught me since I was young.
To this day I tell about the miracles You do....
I will tell the children about Your power;
I will tell those who live after me about Your might.

PSALM 71:17-18 NCV

The Lord Counsels Me

This Is the Day

This is the day the Lord has made;
let us rejoice and be glad in it.

PSALM 118:24 NIV

I've thrown myself headlong into Your arms—
I'm celebrating Your rescue.
I'm singing at the top of my lungs,
I'm so full of answered prayers.

PSALM 13:5-6 THE MESSAGE

Happy are those who hear the joyful call to worship,
for they will walk in the light of Your presence, Lord.
They rejoice all day long in Your wonderful reputation.
They exult in Your righteousness.

PSALM 89:15-16 NLT

Let the skies rejoice and the earth be glad;
let the sea and everything in it shout.
Let the fields and everything in them rejoice.
Then all the trees of the forest will sing for joy
before the Lord, because He is coming.

PSALM 96:11-13 NCV

This Is the Day

The Lord Gives Me Strength and a Song

Thank the Lord because He is good.
His love continues forever.
Let the people of Israel say,
"His love continues forever."
Let the family of Aaron say,
"His love continues forever."
Let those who respect the Lord say,
"His love continues forever."
I was in trouble, so I called to the Lord.
The Lord answered me and set me free.
I will not be afraid, because the Lord is with me.
People can't do anything to me.
The Lord is with me to help me,
so I will see my enemies defeated.
It is better to trust the Lord
than to trust people....
All the nations surrounded me,
but I defeated them in the name of the Lord....
The Lord gives me strength and a song.
He has saved me.

PSALM 118:1-8, 10, 14 NCV

The Lord Gives Me Strength and a Song.

Let Everything that has Breath Praise the Lord

Praise the Lord.
Praise God in His sanctuary;
praise Him in His mighty heavens.
Praise Him for His acts of power;
praise Him for His surpassing greatness.
Praise Him with the sounding of the trumpet,
praise Him with the harp and lyre,
praise Him with tambourine and dancing,
praise Him with the strings and flute,
praise Him with the clash of cymbals,
praise Him with resounding cymbals.
Let everything that has breath praise the Lord.
Praise the Lord.

PSALM 150:1-6 NIV

Kings of the earth and all nations,
princes and all rulers of the earth,
young men and women,
old people and children.
Praise the Lord,
because He alone is great.
He is more wonderful than heaven and earth.

PSALM 148:11-13 NCV

Let Everything that has Breath Praise the Lord

He Guards the Faithful

Step down out of heaven, God;
ignite volcanoes in the hearts of the mountains.
Hurl Your lightnings in every direction;
shoot Your arrows this way and that.
Reach all the way from sky to sea:
pull me out of the ocean of hate,
out of the grip of those barbarians
Who lie through their teeth,
who shake your hand
then knife you in the back.
O God, let me sing a new song to You,
let me play it on a twelve-string guitar—
A song to the God who saved the king,
the God who rescued David, His servant.

PSALM 144:5-10 THE MESSAGE

Let those who love the Lord hate evil,
for He guards the lives of His faithful ones
and delivers them from the hand of the wicked.

PSALM 97:10 NIV

He Guards the Faithful

The Lord, Our Shield

Though a mighty army surrounds me,
my heart will not be afraid.
Even if I am attacked,
I will remain confident.
The one thing I ask of the Lord—
the thing I seek most—
is to live in the house of the Lord all the days of my life,
delighting in the Lord's perfections
and meditating in His Temple.

PSALM 27:3-4 NLT

No king is saved by his great army.
No warrior escapes by his great strength....
But the Lord looks after those who fear Him,
those who put their hope in His love....
So our hope is in the Lord.
He is our help, our shield to protect us.
We rejoice in Him,
because we trust His holy name.
Lord, show Your love to us
as we put our hope in You.

PSALM 33:16, 18, 20-22 NCV

The Lord, Our Shield

He Leads the Humble

*B*lessed is the man who fears the Lord,
Who delights greatly in His commandments.
His descendants will be mighty on earth;
The generation of the upright will be blessed.
Wealth and riches will be in his house,
And his righteousness endures forever.

PSALM 112:1-3 NKJV

*T*he Lord is good and does what is right;
He shows the proper path to those who go astray.
He leads the humble in doing right,
teaching them His way.
The Lord leads with unfailing love and faithfulness
all who keep His covenant and obey His demands.

PSALM 25:8-10 NLT

O Lord, You are so good, so ready to forgive,
so full of unfailing love for all who ask for Your help.

PSALM 86:5 NLT

He Leads the Humble

The Generosity of God

I am the Lord your God,
who brought you up out of Egypt.
Open wide your mouth and I will fill it.

PSALM 81:10 NIV

Your strength, God, is the king's strength....
You filled his arms with gifts;
You gave him a right royal welcome....
You lifted him high and bright as a cumulus cloud,
then dressed him in rainbow colors.
You pile blessings on him;
You make him glad when You smile.
Is it any wonder the king loves God?
that he's sticking with the Best?

PSALM 21:1-3, 5-7 THE MESSAGE

For the Lord God is a sun and shield;
The Lord gives grace and glory;
No good thing does He withhold from those who walk uprightly.
O Lord of hosts,
How blessed is the man who trusts in You!

PSALM 84:11-12 NASB

The Generosity of God

....

....

....

....

....

....

....

....

....

....

....

....

....

....

....

....

....

The Lord is My Strength

The Lord is my light and my salvation—
whom shall I fear?
The Lord is the stronghold of my life—
of whom shall I be afraid?

PSALM 27:1 NIV

I will extol You, O Lord, for You have lifted me up,
And have not let my foes rejoice over me.
O Lord my God, I cried out to You,
And You healed me.
O Lord, You brought my soul up from the grave;
You have kept me alive, that I should not go down to the pit.

PSALM 30:1-3 NKJV

May all who search for You
be filled with joy and gladness in You.
May those who love Your salvation
repeatedly shout, "The Lord is great!"
As for me...let the Lord keep me in His thoughts.
You are my helper and my savior.

PSALM 40:16-17 NLT

The Lord is My Strength

Forgiveness

Help us, O God our Savior,
for the glory of Your name;
deliver us and forgive our sins
for Your name's sake.

PSALM 79:9 NIV

The Lord is gracious and full of compassion,
Slow to anger and great in mercy.
The Lord is good to all,
And His tender mercies are over all His works.

PSALM 145:8-9 NKJV

Happy is the person
whose sins are forgiven
whose wrongs are pardoned.

PSALM 32:1 NCV

God, be merciful to me
because You are loving.
Because You are always ready to be merciful,
wipe out all my wrongs.

PSALM 51:1 NCV

Forgiveness

_____
_____
_____
_____
_____
_____
_____
_____
_____
_____
_____
_____
_____
_____
_____
_____

Wait Patiently

Rest in the Lord, and wait patiently for Him....
Those who wait on the Lord,
They shall inherit the earth.

PSALM 37:7, 9 NKJV

Let all that I am wait quietly before God,
for my hope is in Him.
He alone is my rock and my salvation,
my fortress where I will not be shaken.
My victory and honor come from God alone.
He is my refuge, a rock where no enemy can reach me.
O my people, trust in Him at all times.
Pour out your heart to Him,
for God is our refuge.

PSALM 62:5-8 NLT

I am still confident of this:
I will see the goodness of the Lord
in the land of the living.
Wait for the Lord;
be strong and take heart
and wait for the Lord.

PSALM 27:13-14 NIV

Wait Patiently

Our Dwelling Place

Lord, You have been our dwelling place in all generations.
Before the mountains were brought forth,
Or ever You had formed the earth and the world,
Even from everlasting to everlasting, You are God.

PSALM 90:1-2 NKJV

Who is the man that fears the Lord?
Him shall He teach in the way He chooses.
He himself shall dwell in prosperity,
And his descendants shall inherit the earth.
The secret of the Lord is with those who fear Him,
And He will show them His covenant.

PSALM 25:12-14 NKJV

He who dwells in the shelter of the Most High
Will abide in the shadow of the Almighty.
I will say of the Lord, "He is my refuge and my fortress,
My God, in whom I trust."

PSALM 91:1-2 NASB

Our Dwelling Place

Be Exalted, O Lord!

Be still, and know that I am God;
I will be exalted among the nations,
I will be exalted in the earth!

PSALM 46:10 NKJV

Be exalted, O Lord, in Your strength;
we will sing and praise Your might.

PSALM 21:13 NIV

Praise the Lord, because He alone is great.
He is more wonderful than heaven and earth.
God has given His people a king.
He should be praised by all who belong to Him;
He should be praised by the Israelites,
the people closest to His heart.

PSALM 148:13-14 NCV

For You, Lord, are most high above all the earth;
You are exalted far above all gods.

PSALM 97:9 NKJV

Be Exalted, O Lord!

The Giver of Wisdom

So teach us to number our days,
That we may gain a heart of wisdom.

PSALM 90:12 NKJV

Turn my heart toward Your statutes
and not toward selfish gain.
Turn my eyes away from worthless things;
preserve my life according to Your word.

PSALM 119:36-37 NIV

Fear of the Lord is the foundation of true wisdom.
All who obey His commandments will grow in wisdom.
Praise Him forever!

PSALM 111:10 NLT

Surely You desire truth in the inner parts;
You teach me wisdom in the inmost place.

PSALM 51:6 NIV

The Giver of Wisdom

Hold My Hand, Lord

The steps of a man are established by the Lord,
And He delights in his way.
When he falls, he will not be hurled headlong,
because the Lord is the One who holds his hand.

PSALM 37:23-24 NASB

You, O Lord, are a shield around me;
You are my glory, the One who holds my head high.

PSALM 3:3 NLT

I am always with You;
You have held my hand.
You guide me with Your advice,
and later You will receive me in honor.
I have no one in heaven but You;
I want nothing on earth besides You.
My body and my mind may become weak,
but God is my strength.
He is mine forever....
I am close to God, and that is good.
The Lord God is my protection.
I will tell all that You have done.

PSALM 73:23-26, 28 NCV

Hold My Hand, Lord

He Delivered Me from all My Fears

When I said, "My foot is slipping,"
Your love, O Lord, supported me.
When anxiety was great within me,
Your consolation brought joy to my soul.

PSALM 94:18-19 NIV

Great peace have they who love Your law,
and nothing can make them stumble.

PSALM 119:165 NIV

I sought the Lord, and He answered me;
He delivered me from all my fears.
Those who look to Him are radiant;
their faces are never covered with shame.
This poor man called, and the Lord heard him;
He saved him out of all his troubles.

PSALM 34:4-6 NIV

The Lord will give strength to His people;
The Lord will bless His people with peace.

PSALM 29:11 NKJV

He Delivered Me from all My Fears

From the Rising of the Sun

Praise, O servants of the Lord,
Praise the name of the Lord.
Blessed be the name of the Lord
From this time forth and forever.
From the rising of the sun to its setting
The name of the Lord is to be praised.

PSALM 113:1-3 NASB

Both the day and the night are Yours;
You made the sun and the moon.
You set all the limits on the earth;
You created summer and winter.

PSALM 74:16-17 NCV

The heavens proclaim the glory of God.
The skies display His craftsmanship.
Day after day they continue to speak;
night after night they make Him known.
They speak without a sound or word;
their voice is never heard.

PSALM 19:1-3 NLT

From the Rising of the Sun

Come Before His Presence With Singing

Shout joyfully to the Lord, all the earth.
Serve the Lord with gladness;
Come before Him with joyful singing.
Know that the Lord Himself is God;
It is He who has made us, and not we ourselves;
We are His people and the sheep of His pasture.
Enter His gates with thanksgiving
And His courts with praise
Give thanks to Him, bless His name.
For the Lord is good;
His lovingkindness is everlasting
And His faithfulness to all generations.

PSALM 100:1-5 NASB

I will praise You, O Lord, with all my heart;
I will tell of all Your wonders.
I will be glad and rejoice in You;
I will sing praise to Your name, O Most High.

PSALM 9:1-2 NIV

Come Before His Presence With Singing

Hear My Prayer

Hear my prayer, O Lord God Almighty;
listen to me, O God of Jacob.
Look upon our shield, O God;
look with favor on Your anointed one.

PSALM 84:8-9 NIV

Answer me when I call, O God of my righteousness!
You have relieved me in my distress;
Be gracious to me and hear my prayer.

PSALM 4:1 NASB

The Lord is a shelter for the oppressed,
a refuge in times of trouble.
Those who know Your name trust in You,
for You, O Lord, do not abandon those who search for You.
Sing praises to the Lord who reigns in Jerusalem.
Tell the world about His unforgettable deeds....
He does not ignore the cries of those who suffer.

PSALM 9:9-12 NLT

Hear My Prayer

I Will Not Be Afraid

God is our refuge and strength,
A very present help in trouble.
Therefore we will not fear,
Even though the earth be removed,
And though the mountains be carried
into the midst of the sea;
Though its waters roar and be troubled,
Though the mountains shake with its swelling.

PSALM 46:1-3 NKJV

Be merciful to me, O God, for men hotly pursue me;
all day long they press their attack.
My slanderers pursue me all day long;
many are attacking me in their pride.
When I am afraid,
I will trust in You.
In God, whose word I praise,
in God I trust; I will not be afraid.
What can mortal man do to me?

PSALM 56:1-4 NIV

I Will Not Be Afraid

My Deliverer

The Lord is your keeper;
The Lord is your shade on your right hand.
The sun will not smite you by day,
Nor the moon by night.
The Lord will protect you from all evil;
He will keep your soul.
The Lord will guard your going out and your coming in
From this time forth and forever.

PSALM 121:5-8 NASB

Show Your marvelous lovingkindness by Your right hand,
O You who save those who trust in You
From those who rise up against them.
Keep me as the apple of Your eye;
Hide me under the shadow of Your wings.

PSALM 17:7-8 NKJV

Through God we will do valiantly,
And it is He who shall tread down our adversaries.

PSALM 108:13 NASB

God's strong name is our help,
the same God who made heaven and earth.

PSALM 124:8 THE MESSAGE

My Deliverer

He Owns Each Day

"Lord, remind me how brief my time on earth will be.
Remind me that my days are numbered—
how fleeting my life is.
You have made my life no longer than the width of my hand.
My entire lifetime is just a moment to You;
at best, each of us is but a breath."
We are merely moving shadows,
and all our busy rushing ends in nothing.
We heap up wealth,
not knowing who will spend it.
And so, Lord, where do I put my hope?
My only hope is in You.

PSALM 39:4-7 NLT

He asked life from You, and You gave it to him—
Length of days forever and ever.

PSALM 21:4 NKJV

For You, a thousand years are as a passing day,
as brief as a few night hours.

PSALM 90:4 NLT

He Owns Each Day

Merciful Savior

I love the Lord because He hears my voice
and my prayer for mercy.
Because He bends down to listen,
I will pray as long as I have breath!
Death wrapped its ropes around me;
the terrors of the grave overtook me.
I saw only trouble and sorrow.
Then I called on the name of the Lord:
"Please, Lord, save me!"
How kind the Lord is! How good He is!
So merciful, this God of ours!

PSALM 116:1-5 NLT

The Lord upholds all who fall,
And raises up all who are bowed down.

PSALM 145:14 NKJV

He who trusts in the Lord, mercy shall surround him.
Be glad in the Lord and rejoice, you righteous;
And shout for joy, all you upright in heart!

PSALM 32:10-11 NKJV

Merciful Savior

Hope in God

Why are you cast down, O my soul?
And why are you disquieted within me?
Hope in God, for I shall yet praise Him
For the help of His countenance....
Deep calls unto deep at the noise of Your waterfalls;
All Your waves and billows have gone over me.
The Lord will command His lovingkindness in the daytime,
And in the night His song shall be with me—
A prayer to the God of my life.

PSALM 42:5, 7-8 NKJV

All you who put your hope in the Lord
be strong and brave.

PSALM 31:24 NCV

Happy are those who are helped by the God of Jacob.
Their hope is in the Lord their God.
He made heaven and earth,
the sea and everything in it.
He remains loyal forever.

PSALM 146:5-6 NCV

Hope in God

Your Word Is a Lamp to My Feet

How can a young person live a pure life?
By obeying Your word.
With all my heart I try to obey You.
Don't let me break Your commands.
I have taken Your words to heart
so I would not sin against You.

PSALM 119:9-11 NCV

Because I love Your commands
more than gold, more than pure gold,
and because I consider all Your precepts right,
I hate every wrong path.

PSALM 119:127-128 NIV

Your word is a lamp to my feet
and a light for my path.

PSALM 119:105 NIV

Your Word Is a Lamp to My Feet

The City of the Great King

Great is the Lord, and greatly to be praised,
In the city of our God, His holy mountain.
Beautiful in elevation, the joy of the whole earth,
Is Mount Zion in the far north,
The city of the great King.
God, in her palaces,
Has made Himself known as a stronghold....
In the city of the Lord of hosts, in the city of our God;
God will establish her forever.
We have thought on Your lovingkindness, O God,
In the midst of Your temple.
As is Your name, O God,
So is Your praise to the ends of the earth;
Your right hand is full of righteousness.

PSALM 48:1-3, 8-10 NASB

There is a river that brings joy to the city of God,
the holy place where God Most High lives.
God is in that city, and so it will not be shaken.

PSALM 46:4-5 NCV

The City of the Great King

His Love to Me Is Wonderful

How great is Your goodness
that You have stored up for those who fear You,
that You have given to those who trust You.
You do this for all to see.
You protect them by Your presence
from what people plan against them.
You shelter them from evil words.
Praise the Lord.
His love to me was wonderful
when my city was attacked.
In my distress, I said,
"God cannot see me!"
But You heard my prayer
when I cried out to You for help.

Psalm 31:19-22 ncv

Answer my prayers, O Lord,
for Your unfailing love is wonderful.
Take care of me,
for Your mercy is so plentiful.

Psalm 69:16 nlt

His Love to Me Is Wonderful

_____

_____

_____

_____

_____

_____

_____

_____

_____

_____

_____

_____

_____

_____

_____

Only by Your Power

Unless the Lord builds the house,
They labor in vain who build it;
Unless the Lord guards the city,
The watchman keeps awake in vain.

PSALM 127:1 NASB

Only by Your power can we push back our enemies;
only in Your name can we trample our foes.
I do not trust in my bow;
I do not count on my sword to save me.
You are the one who gives us victory.

PSALM 44:5-7 NLT

Blessed be the Lord God, the God of Israel,
Who alone works wonders.
And blessed be His glorious name forever;
And may the whole earth be filled with His glory.

PSALM 72:18-19 NASB

Only by Your Power

My Soul Thirsts for God

As a deer thirsts for streams of water,
so I thirst for You, God.
I thirst for the living God.

PSALM 42:1-2 NCV

O God, You are my God;
Early will I seek You;
My soul thirsts for You;
My flesh longs for You
In a dry and thirsty land
Where there is no water.
So I have looked for You in the sanctuary,
To see Your power and Your glory.
Because Your lovingkindness is better than life,
My lips shall praise You.
Thus I will bless You while I live;
I will lift up my hands in Your name.
My soul shall be satisfied as with marrow and fatness,
And my mouth shall praise You with joyful lips.

PSALM 63:1-5 NKJV

My Soul Thirsts for God

My Soul Waits for the Lord

My soul waits for the Lord
more than watchmen wait for the morning,
more than watchmen wait for the morning.
O Israel, put your hope in the Lord,
for with the Lord is unfailing love
and with Him is full redemption.

PSALM 130:6-7 NIV

I am waiting for You to save me, Lord.
I will obey Your commands.
I obey Your rules,
and I love them very much.

PSALM 119:166-167 NCV

I look to You, heaven-dwelling God, look up to You for help.
Like servants, alert to their master's commands,
like a maiden attending her lady,
We're watching and waiting, holding our breath,
awaiting Your word of mercy.

PSALM 123:1-2 THE MESSAGE

I wait for the Lord to help me,
and I trust His word.

PSALM 130:5 NCV

My Soul Waits for the Lord

Sing Praises

Clap your hands, all you nations;
shout to God with cries of joy.
How awesome is the Lord Most High,
the great King over all the earth!...
God has ascended amid shouts of joy,
the Lord amid the sounding of trumpets.
Sing praises to God, sing praises;
sing praises to our King, sing praises.

PSALM 47:1-2, 5-6 NIV

It is good to praise You with the ten-stringed lyre
and with the soft-sounding harp.
Lord, You have made me happy by what You have done;
I will sing for joy about what Your hands have done.
Lord, You have done such great things!
How deep are Your thoughts!

PSALM 92:3-5 NCV

Sing Praises

Beyond Understanding

*H*e counts the stars
and assigns each a name.
Our Lord is great, with limitless strength;
we'll never comprehend what He knows and does.

Psalm 147:4-5 the message

*Y*our knowledge is amazing to me;
it is more than I can understand.

Psalm 139:6 ncv

*G*reat is the Lord, and greatly to be praised;
And His greatness is unsearchable.

Psalm 145:3 nkjv

*B*ut as for me, I will always have hope;
I will praise You more and more.
My mouth will tell of Your righteousness,
of Your salvation all day long,
though I know not its measure.

Psalm 71:14-15 niv

Beyond Understanding

For When He Spoke, the World Began

The Lord merely spoke,
and the heavens were created.
He breathed the word,
and all the stars were born.
He assigned the sea its boundaries
and locked the oceans in vast reservoirs.
Let the whole world fear the Lord,
and let everyone stand in awe of Him.
For when He spoke, the world began!

PSALM 33:6-9 NLT

He spoke the word, and there they were!
He set them in place
from all time to eternity;
He gave His orders, and that's it!
Praise God from earth,
you sea dragons, you fathomless ocean deeps;
Fire and hail, snow and ice,
hurricanes obeying His orders;
Mountains and all hills,
apple orchards and cedar forests;
Wild beasts and herds of cattle,
snakes, and birds in flight.

PSALM 148:5-10 THE MESSAGE

For When He Spoke, the World Began

Generations Will Praise Him

One generation shall praise Your works to another,
And shall declare Your mighty acts.

PSALM 145:4 NKJV

Give ear, O my people, to my law;
Incline your ears to the words of my mouth.
I will open my mouth in a parable;...
Which we have heard and known,
And our fathers have told us.
We will not hide them from their children,
Telling to the generation to come the praises of the Lord,
And His strength and His wonderful works that He has done....
That the generation to come might know them,
The children who would be born,
That they may arise and declare them to their children,
That they may set their hope in God,
And not forget the works of God,
But keep His commandments.

PSALM 78:1-4, 6-7 NKJV

Your name, O Lord, endures forever;
Your fame, O Lord, is known to every generation.

PSALM 135:13 NLT

Generations Will Praise Him

You Are My Hiding Place

I run to You, God; I run for dear life....
Get down on my level and listen....
Your granite cave a hiding place,
Your high cliff [nest] a place of safety.
You're my cave to hide in,
my cliff to climb.
Be my safe leader,
be my true mountain guide.
Free me from hidden traps;
I want to hide in You.
I've put my life in Your hands.
You won't drop me,
You'll never let me down.

PSALM 31:1-5 THE MESSAGE

You are my hiding place;
You shall preserve me from trouble;
You shall surround me with songs of deliverance.

PSALM 32:7 NKJV

You Are My Hiding Place

You Know Me
Inside and Out

Lord, You have examined me
and know all about me.
You know when I sit down and when I get up.
You know my thoughts before I think them.
You know where I go and where I lie down.
You know everything I do.
Lord, even before I say a word,
You already know it....
You made my whole being;
You formed me in my mother's body.
I praise You because You made me in an amazing and wonderful way.
What You have done is wonderful.
I know this very well.
You saw my bones being formed
as I took shape in my mother's body.

PSALM 139:1-4, 13-15 NCV

I obey Your precepts and Your statutes,
for all my ways are known to You.

PSALM 119:168 NIV

You Know Me Inside and Out

Call Out to God

Help me, O Lord my God!
Save me because of Your unfailing love.

PSALM 109:26 NLT

Don't turn a deaf ear when I call You, God.
If all I get from You is
deafening silence,
I'd be better off
in the Black Hole.
I'm letting You know what I need,
calling out for help
And lifting my arms
toward Your inner sanctum.

PSALM 28:1-2 THE MESSAGE

In times of trouble, may the Lord answer your cry.
May the name of the God of Jacob keep you safe from all harm.
May He send you help from His sanctuary
and strengthen you from Jerusalem.
May He remember all your gifts
and look favorably on your burnt offerings.

PSALM 20:1-3 NLT

Call Out to God

The Lord Is Our Refuge

But let all who take refuge in You rejoice;
let them sing joyful praises forever.
Spread Your protection over them,
that all who love Your name may be filled with joy.
For You bless the godly, O Lord;
You surround them with Your shield of love.

PSALM 5:11-12 NLT

He will cover you with His feathers,
and under His wings you will find refuge;
His faithfulness will be your shield and rampart.

PSALM 91:4 NIV

I love You, Lord. You are my strength.
The Lord is my rock, my protection, my Savior.
My God is my rock.
I can run to Him for safety.
He is my shield and my saving strength, my defender.
I will call to the Lord, who is worthy of praise,
and I will be saved from my enemies.

PSALM 18:1-3 NCV

The Lord Is Our Refuge

I Will Sing of Your Love and Fairness

Declare me innocent, O Lord,
for I have acted with integrity;
I have trusted in the Lord without wavering.
Put me on trial, Lord, and cross-examine me.
Test my motives and my heart.
For I am always aware of Your unfailing love,
and I have lived according to Your truth.

PSALM 26:1-3 NLT

I will sing of Your love and fairness;
Lord, I will sing praises to You.
I will be careful to live an innocent life.
When will You come to me?
I will live an innocent life in my house.

PSALM 101:1-2 NCV

As for me, You uphold me in my integrity,
And You set me in Your presence forever.

PSALM 41:12 NASB

I Will Sing of Your Love and Fairness

The Lord's Everlasting Love

From everlasting to everlasting
the Lord's love is with those who fear Him,
and His righteousness with their children's children—
with those who keep His covenant
and remember to obey His precepts.

Psalm 103:17-18 niv

I will be glad and rejoice in Your unfailing love,
for You have seen my troubles,
and You care about the anguish of my soul.
You have not handed me over to my enemies
but have set me in a safe place.

Psalm 31:7-8 nlt

You, O Lord, are a compassionate and gracious God,
slow to anger, abounding in love and faithfulness.

Psalm 86:15 niv

I will say, "Your love continues forever;
Your loyalty goes on and on like the sky."

Psalm 89:2 ncv

The Lord's Everlasting Love

Everything Belongs to God

The earth is the Lord's, and everything in it,
the world, and all who live in it;
for He founded it upon the seas
and established it upon the waters.
Who may ascend the hill of the Lord?
Who may stand in His holy place?
He who has clean hands and a pure heart,
who does not lift up his soul to an idol
or swear by what is false.
He will receive blessing from the Lord
and vindication from God his Savior.
Such is the generation of those who seek Him,
who seek Your face, O God of Jacob.

PSALM 18:46 NKJV

The heavens are Yours, and the earth is Yours;
everything in the world is Yours—You created it all.

PSALM 89:11 NLT

Everything Belongs to God

Blessed Are the Peacemakers

How wonderful and pleasant it is
when brothers live together in harmony!
For harmony is as precious as the anointing oil
that was poured over Aaron's head,
that ran down his beard
and onto the border of his robe.

PSALM 133:1-2 NLT

Lord, help me control my tongue;
help me be careful about what I say.

PSALM 141:3 NCV

I said, "I will be careful how I act
and will not sin by what I say."

PSALM 39:1 NCV

Depart from evil and do good;
Seek peace and pursue it.
The eyes of the Lord are on the righteous,
And His ears are open to their cry.

PSALM 34:14-15 NKJV

Blessed Are the Peacemakers

He Sets Me on My High Places

May He give you what you want
and make all your plans succeed,
and we will shout for joy when you succeed,
and we will raise a flag in the name of our God.
May the Lord give you all that you ask for.

PSALM 20:4-5 NCV

It is God who arms me with strength,
And makes my way perfect.
He makes my feet like the feet of deer,
And sets me on my high places....
You have also given me the shield of Your salvation;
Your right hand has held me up,
Your gentleness has made me great.
You enlarged my path under me,
So my feet did not slip.

PSALM 18:32-33, 35-36 NKJV

My steps have held fast to Your paths
My feet have not slipped.
I have called upon You, for You will answer me, O God.

PSALM 17:5-6 NASB

He Sets Me on My High Places

Behold His Works

The earth is full of Your possessions.
There is the sea, great and broad,
In which are swarms without number,
Animals both small and great.
There the ships move along,
And Leviathan, which You have formed to sport in it.
They all wait for You
To give them their food in due season.
You give to them, they gather it up;
You open Your hand, they are satisfied with good.
You hide Your face, they are dismayed;
You take away their spirit, they expire
And return to their dust.
You send forth Your Spirit, they are created;
And You renew the face of the ground.
Let the glory of the Lord endure forever;
Let the Lord be glad in His works.

PSALM 104:24-31 NASB

Behold His Works

Sing a New Song!

Oh, sing to the Lord a new song!
Sing to the Lord, all the earth.
Sing to the Lord, bless His name;
Proclaim the good news of His salvation from day to day.
Declare His glory among the nations,
His wonders among all peoples.
For the Lord is great and greatly to be praised;
He is to be feared above all gods.
For all the gods of the peoples are idols,
But the Lord made the heavens.
Honor and majesty are before Him;
Strength and beauty are in His sanctuary.

PSALM 96:1-6 NKJV

Hallelujah! O my soul, praise God!
All my life long I'll praise God,
singing songs to my God as long as I live.

PSALM 146:2 THE MESSAGE

Sing a New Song!

Seek Him Morning and Evening

It is good to praise the Lord
and make music to Your name, O Most High,
to proclaim Your love in the morning
and Your faithfulness at night.

Psalm 92:1-2 niv

The Lord has looked down from heaven upon the sons of men
To see if there are any who understand,
Who seek after God.

Psalm 14:2 nasb

Fill us with Your love every morning.
Then we will sing and rejoice all our lives.

Psalm 90:14 ncv

Listen to my cry for help, my King and my God,
for I pray to no one but You.
Listen to my voice in the morning, Lord.
Each morning I bring my requests to You and wait expectantly.

Psalm 5:2-3 nlt

Seek Him Morning and Evening

Our Wise and Loving Sustainer

The young lions roar after their prey
And seek their food from God.
When the sun rises they withdraw
And lie down in their dens.
Man goes forth to his work
And to his labor until evening.
O Lord, how many are Your works!
In wisdom You have made them all;
The earth is full of Your possessions.

PSALM 104:21-24 NASB

They asked, and He brought quail,
And satisfied them with the bread of heaven.
He opened the rock and water flowed out;
It ran in the dry places like a river.
For He remembered His holy word
With Abraham His servant;
And He brought forth His people with joy,
His chosen ones with a joyful shout.

PSALM 105:40-43 NASB

Our Wise and Loving Sustainer

Restore to Me the Joy of Your Salvation

Cleanse me with hyssop, and I will be clean;
wash me, and I will be whiter than snow....
Hide Your face from my sins
and blot out all my iniquity.
Create in me a pure heart, O God,
and renew a steadfast spirit within me.
Do not cast me from Your presence
or take Your Holy Spirit from me.
Restore to me the joy of Your salvation
and grant me a willing spirit, to sustain me.

PSALM 51:7, 9-12 NIV

I have suffered much, O Lord;
restore my life again as You promised.

PSALM 119:107 NLT

Those who sow in tears
Shall reap in joy.
He who continually goes forth weeping,
Bearing seed for sowing,
Shall doubtless come again with rejoicing,
Bringing his sheaves with him.

PSALM 126:5-6 NKJV

Restore to Me the Joy of Your Salvation

When I Consider Your Works

When I consider Your heavens, the work of Your fingers,
The moon and the stars, which You have ordained,
What is man that You are mindful of him,
And the son of man that You visit him?
For You have made him a little lower than the angels,
And You have crowned him with glory and honor.
You have made him to have dominion over the works of Your hands;
You have put all things under his feet,
All sheep and oxen—
Even the beasts of the field,
The birds of the air,
And the fish of the sea
That pass through the paths of the seas.
O Lord, our Lord,
How excellent is Your name in all the earth!

PSALM 8:3-9 NKJV

When I Consider Your Works

The Lord's Promises Are Sure

God's way is perfect.
All the Lord's promises prove true.
He is a shield for all who look to Him for protection.

PSALM 18:30 NLT

Let Your love, God, shape my life
with salvation, exactly as You promised;
Then I'll be able to stand up to mockery
because I trusted Your Word.
Don't ever deprive me of truth, not ever—
Your commandments are what I depend on.
Oh, I'll guard with my life what You've revealed to me,
guard it now, guard it ever;
And I'll stride freely through wide open spaces
as I look for Your truth and Your wisdom;
Then I'll tell the world what I find,
speak out boldly in public, unembarrassed.
I cherish Your commandments—oh, how I love them!—
relishing every fragment of Your counsel.

PSALM 119:41-48 THE MESSAGE

The Lord's promises are pure,
like silver refined in a furnace,
purified seven times over.

PSALM 12:6 NLT

The Lord's Promises Are Sure

....

....

....

....

....

....

....

....

....

....

....

....

....

....

....

I Will Take the Load from Your Shoulders

Now I will take the load from your shoulders;
I will free your hands from their heavy tasks.
You cried to Me in trouble, and I saved you;
I answered out of the thundercloud
and tested your faith.

PSALM 81:6-7 NLT

He has set his love upon Me, therefore I will deliver him;
I will set him on high, because he has known My name.
He shall call upon Me, and I will answer him;
I will be with him in trouble;
I will deliver him and honor him.
With long life I will satisfy him,
And show him My salvation.

PSALM 91:14-16 NKJV

I Will Take the Load from Your Shoulders

Who Can Compare with You, O Lord

All heaven will praise Your great wonders, Lord;
myriads of angels will praise You for Your faithfulness.
For who in all of heaven can compare with the Lord?
What mightiest angel is anything like the Lord?
The highest angelic powers stand in awe of God.
He is far more awesome than all who surround His throne.
O Lord God of Heaven's Armies!
Where is there anyone as mighty as You, O Lord?
You are entirely faithful.

PSALM 89:5-8 NLT

Your throne, O God, is forever and ever;
A scepter of righteousness is the scepter of Your kingdom.
You love righteousness and hate wickedness;
Therefore God, Your God, has anointed You
With the oil of gladness more than Your companions.

PSALM 45:6-7 NKJV

Who Can Compare with You, O Lord

What God Wants

I have no complaint about your sacrifices
or the burnt offerings you constantly offer.
But I do not need the bulls from your barns
or the goats from your pens.
For all the animals of the forest are Mine,
and I own the cattle on a thousand hills.
I know every bird on the mountains,
and all the animals of the field are Mine.
If I were hungry, I would not tell you,
for all the world is Mine and everything in it....
Make thankfulness your sacrifice to God,
and keep the vows you made to the Most High.
Then call on Me when you are in trouble,
and I will rescue you,
and you will give Me glory.

PSALM 50:8-12, 14-15 NLT

What God Wants

Sacrifice of the Heart

I will offer sacrifices of joy in His tabernacle;
I will sing, yes, I will sing praises to the Lord.

PSALM 27:6 NKJV

I will fulfill my vows to You, O God,
and will offer a sacrifice of thanks for Your help.
For You have rescued me from death;
You have kept my feet from slipping.
So now I can walk in Your presence, O God,
in Your life-giving light.

PSALM 56:12-13 NLT

O Lord, open my lips,
and my mouth will declare Your praise.
You do not delight in sacrifice, or I would bring it;
You do not take pleasure in burnt offerings.
The sacrifices of God are a broken spirit;
a broken and contrite heart,
O God, You will not despise.

PSALM 51:15-17 NIV

Sacrifice of the Heart

You Take Care of the Earth

You visit the earth and cause it to overflow;
You greatly enrich it;
The stream of God is full of water;
You prepare their grain, for thus You prepare the earth.
You water its furrows abundantly,
You settle its ridges,
You soften it with showers,
You bless its growth.
You have crowned the year with Your bounty,
And Your paths drip with fatness.
The pastures of the wilderness drip,
And the hills gird themselves with rejoicing.
The meadows are clothed with flocks
And the valleys are covered with grain;
They shout for joy, yes, they sing.

Psalm 65:9-13 nasb

Of old You laid the foundation of the earth,
And the heavens are the work of Your hands.
They will perish, but You will endure....
But You are the same,
And Your years will have no end.

Psalm 102:25-27 nkjv

You Take Care of the Earth

God's Goodness and Peace

The meek shall inherit the earth,
And shall delight themselves in the abundance of peace.

PSALM 37:11 NKJV

I will listen to God the Lord.
He has ordered peace for those who worship Him.
Don't let them go back to foolishness.
God will soon save those who respect Him,
and His glory will be seen in our land.
Love and truth belong to God's people;
goodness and peace will be theirs.
On earth people will be loyal to God,
and God's goodness will shine down from heaven.
The Lord will give His goodness,
and the land will give its crops.
Goodness will go before God
and prepare the way for Him.

PSALM 85:8-9 NASB

Look at those who are honest and good,
for a wonderful future awaits those who love peace.

PSALM 37:37 NLT

God's Goodness and Peace

··

··

··

··

··

··

··

··

··

··

··

··

I will sing of the tender mercies of the Lord forever!
Young and old will hear of Your faithfulness.

Psalm 89:1 nlt